i puffin
love you

HarperCollins*Publishers*
1 London Bridge Street
London SE1 9GF

www.harpercollins.co.uk

First published by HarperCollins*Publishers* 2021

1 3 5 7 9 10 8 6 4 2

Text © HarperCollins*Publishers* 2021
Illustrations © Lydia Kairl

A catalogue record of this book is
available from the British Library

ISBN 978-0-00-845554-5

Printed and bound in Latvia

MIX
Paper from
responsible sources
FSC™ C007454

This book is produced from independently certified FSC™ paper to
ensure responsible forest management.

For more information visit: www.harpercollins.co.uk/green

i puffin
love you

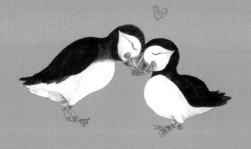

hilarious animal puns
to help you share the love

HarperCollins*Publishers*

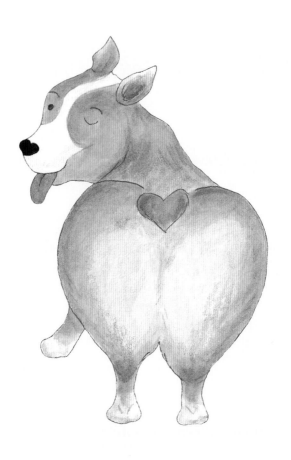

Hey, corgeous!

Some-bunny really loves you

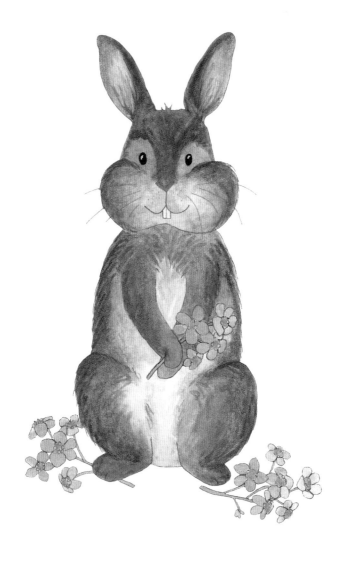

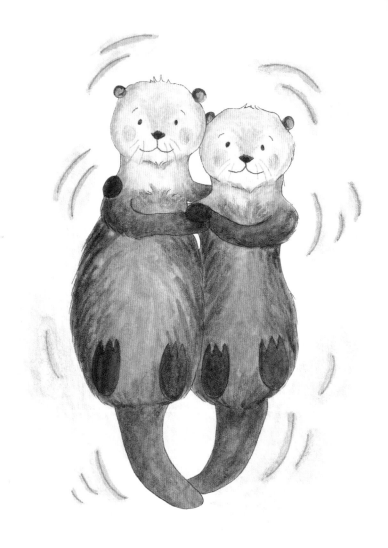

You're my most significant otter

A toucan of my
affection

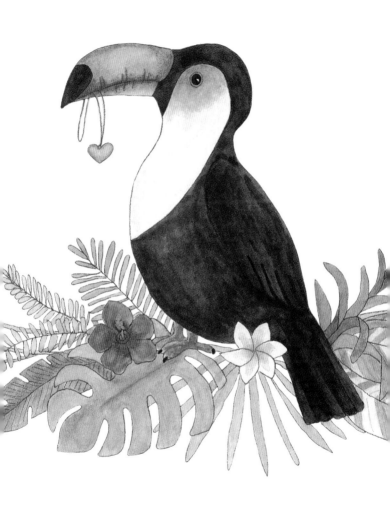

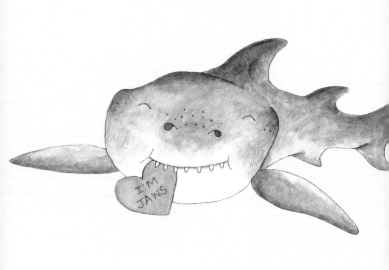

I chews you

You are
dino-mite

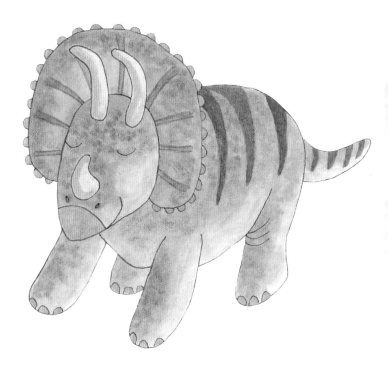

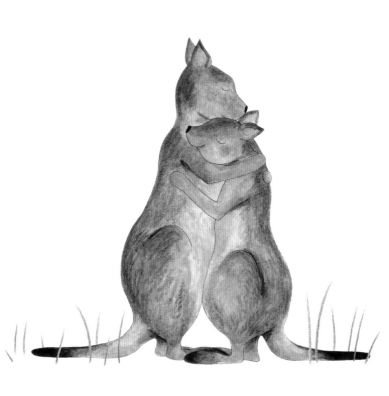

I wallaby by
your side

You're the
bear-y
best

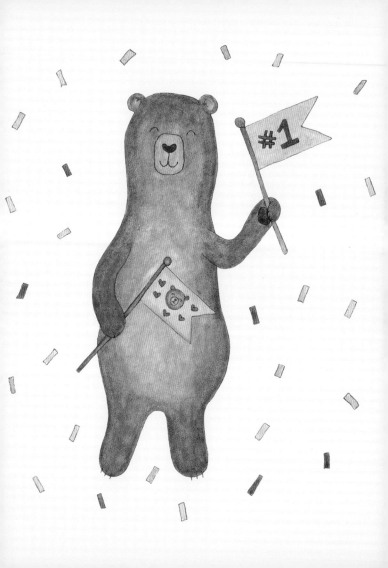

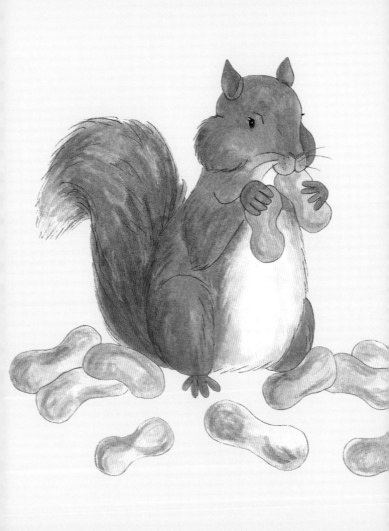

I'm nuts
about you

You're udder-ly perfect

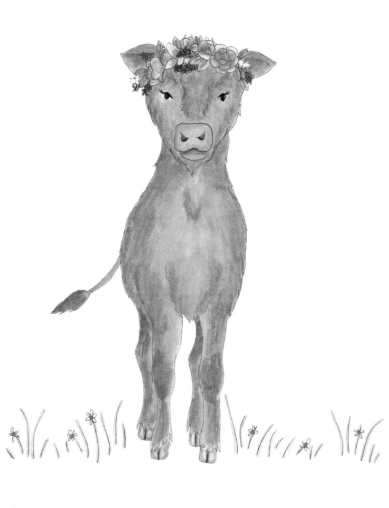

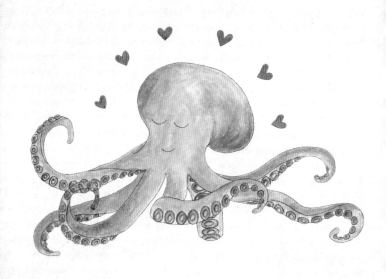

You always
octo-py
my thoughts

Life without you
would be ruff

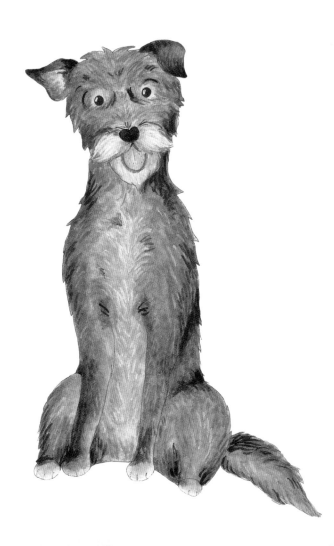

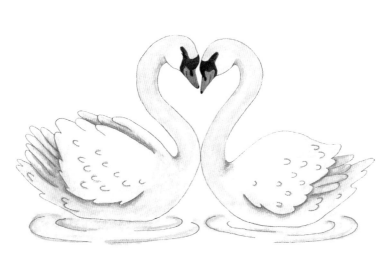

You're the swan
for me

I love spending
koala-ty time
together

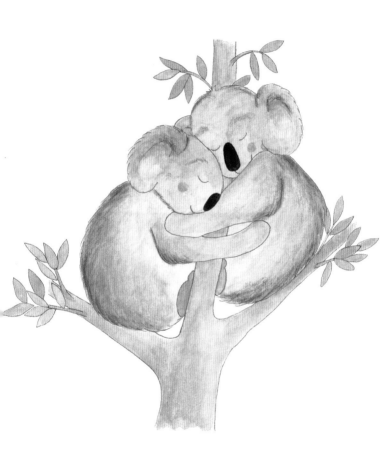

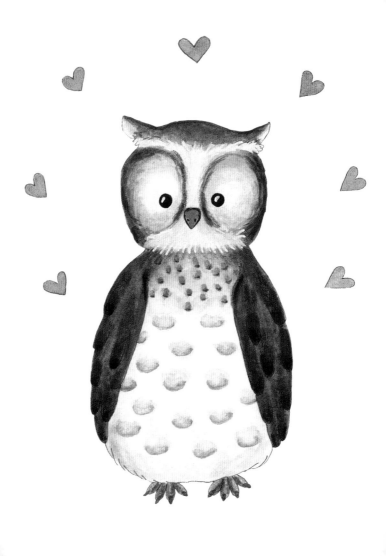

Thank you for
owl-ways
being there for me

You are absolutely
dove-ly

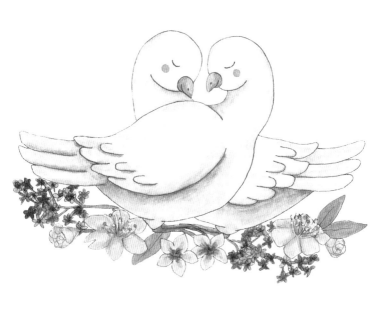

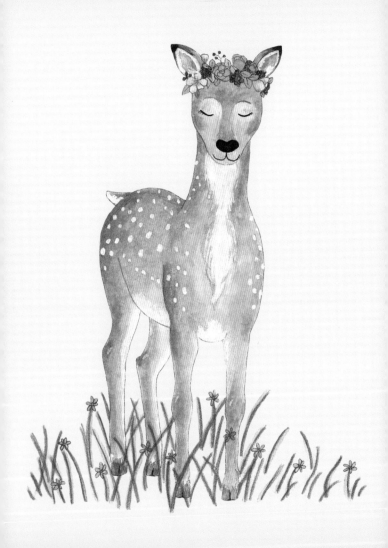

I am very
fawn-ed of you,
my deer

We bee-long together

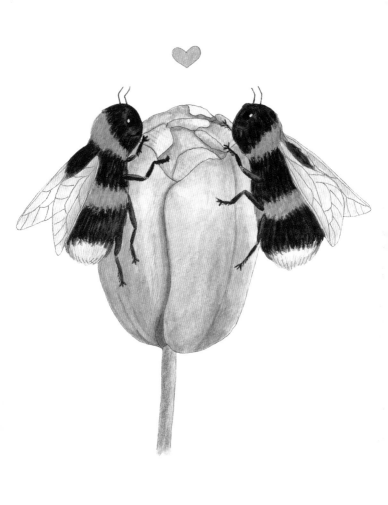

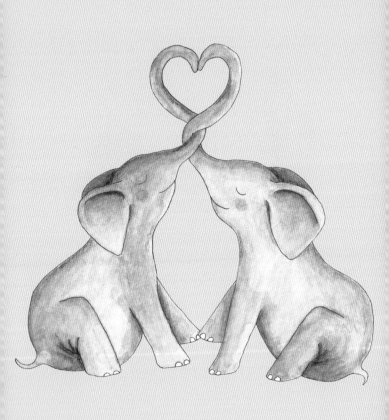

Everything else is irr-elephant when I'm with you

I love you
and rhino you
love me too

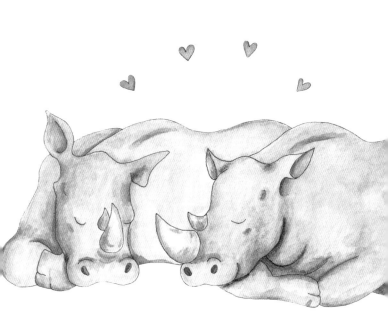

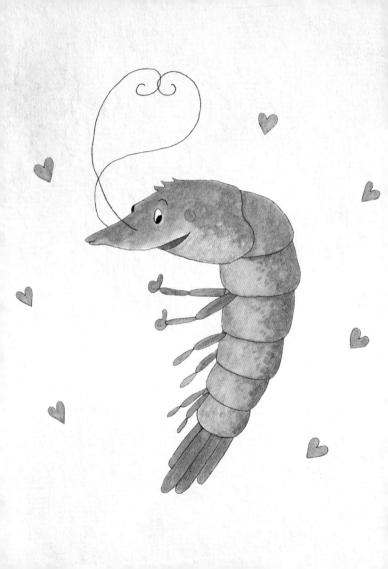

You're shrimp-ly
the best

You are toad-ally amazing

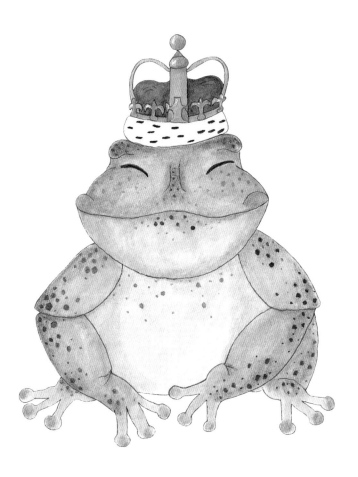

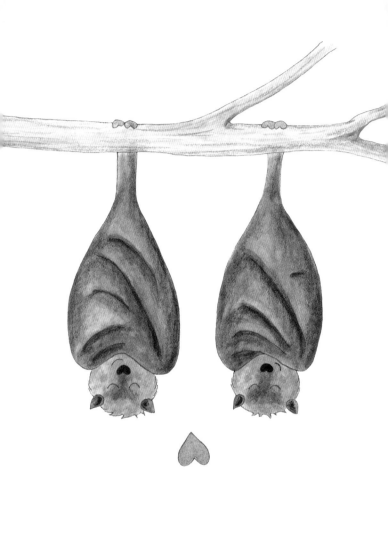

I love hanging
out with you

Ewe complete me

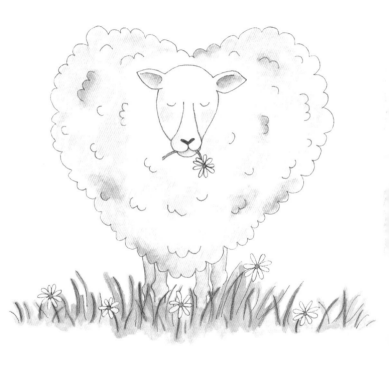

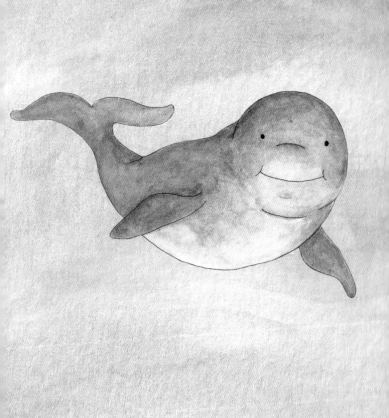

You give my life
porpoise

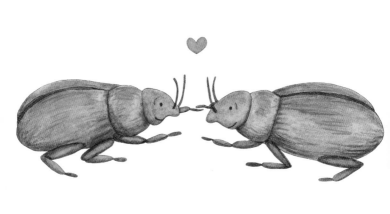

You never bug me

I hippopota-miss
you when you're
away

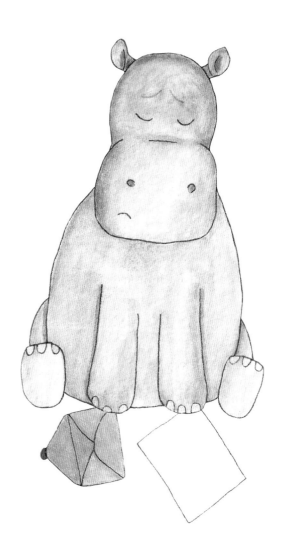

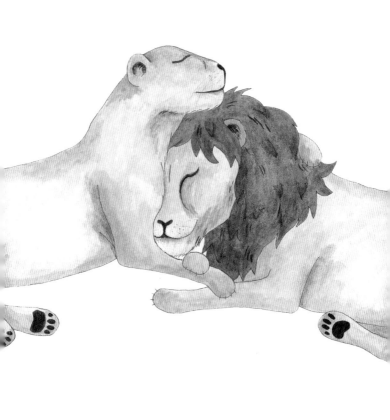

I'd be lion if I said
I didn't love you

You're my
sole-mate

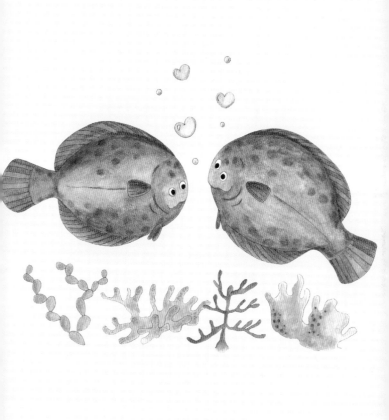

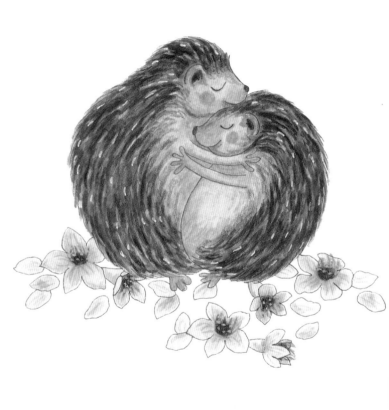

I love our
hedge-hugs

We just clicked

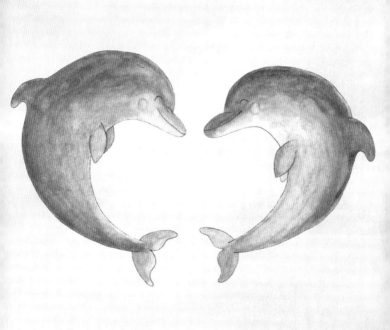

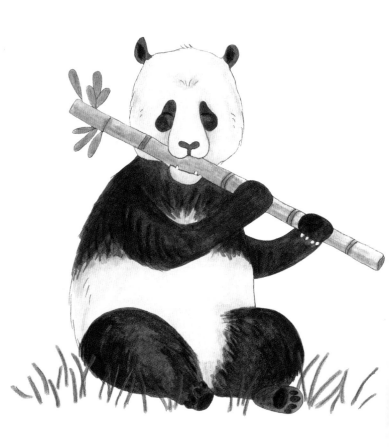

I want to panda to your every need

You hold the kiwi
to my heart

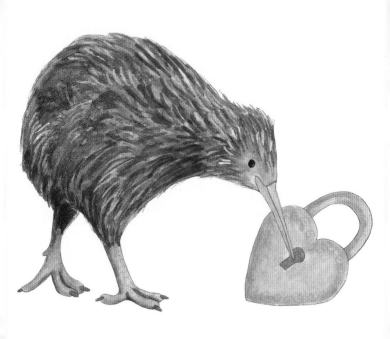

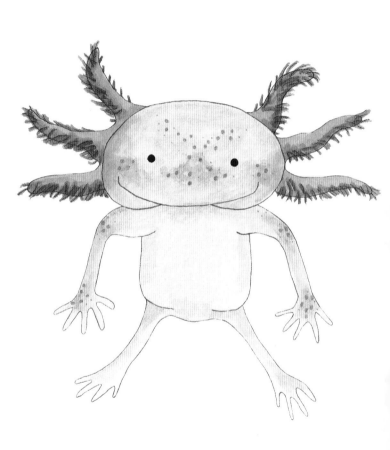

I love you an
axo-lot-l

When we first met,
I gnu you were the
one for me

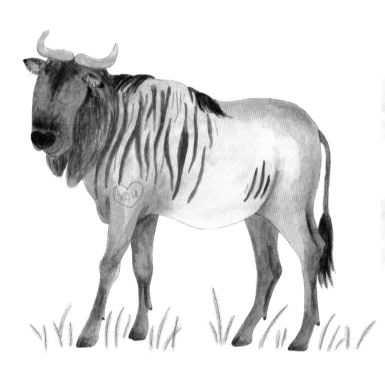

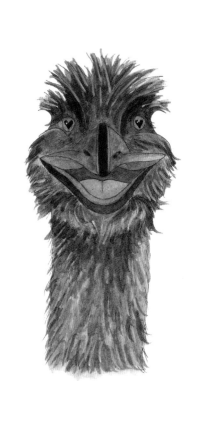

You're always so emu-sing

Life's snow fun
without you

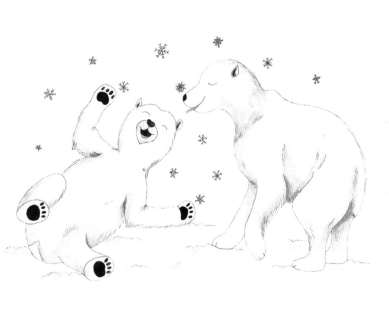

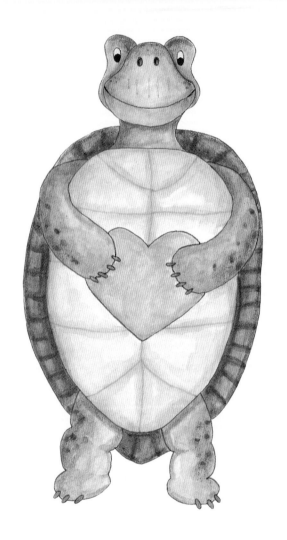

You are turtle-y
adorable

You croc my world

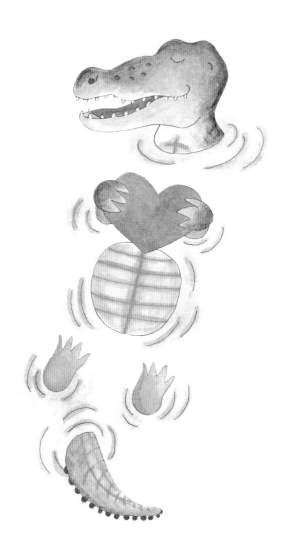

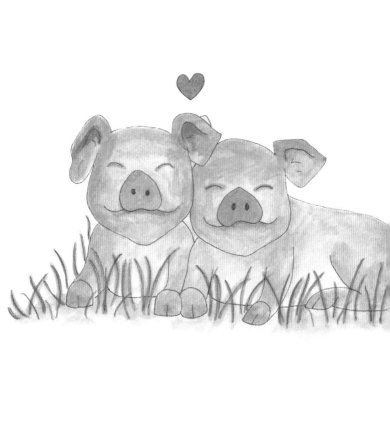

I love you pig
time

You turn my
heart to jelly

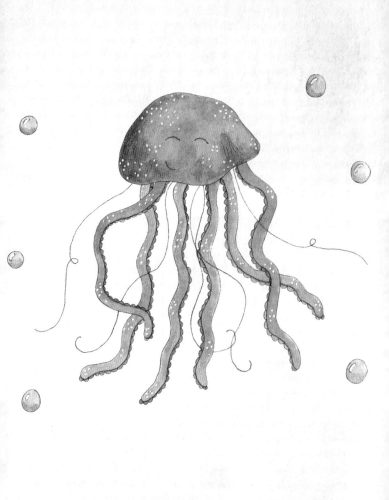

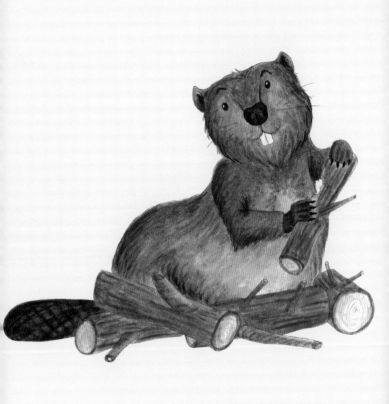

Are you a beaver?
Because dam!

I'm so glad
I've goat you

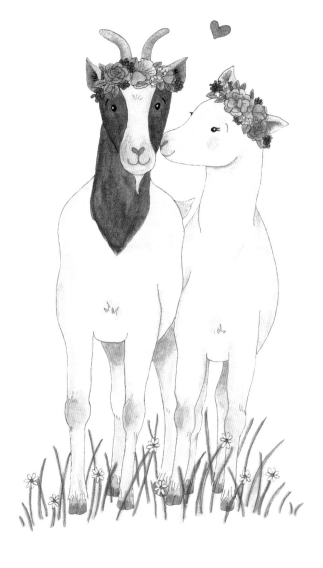

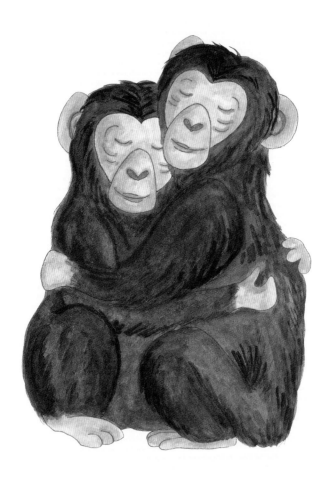

You really are my
prime mate

We go so whale together

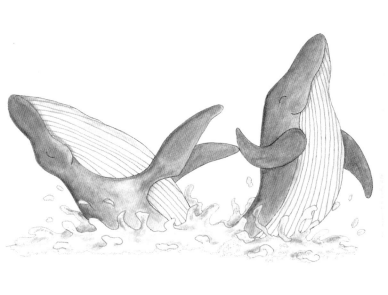

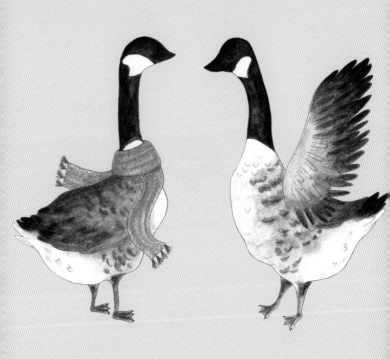

You give me
goosebumps

I porcu-pine for
you when I'm
not with you

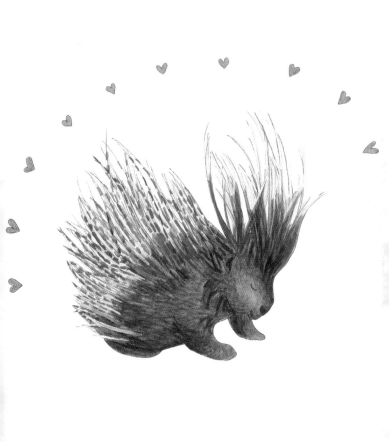

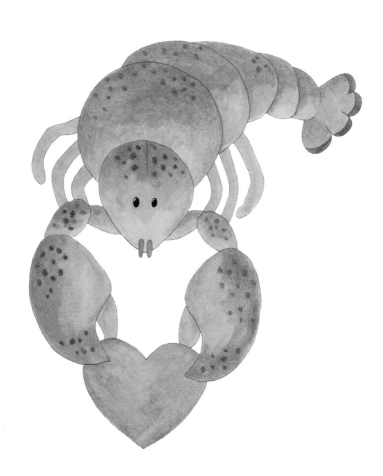

That's a whole
lobster love

I'm head over
eels for you

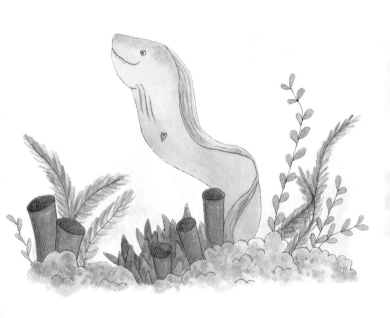

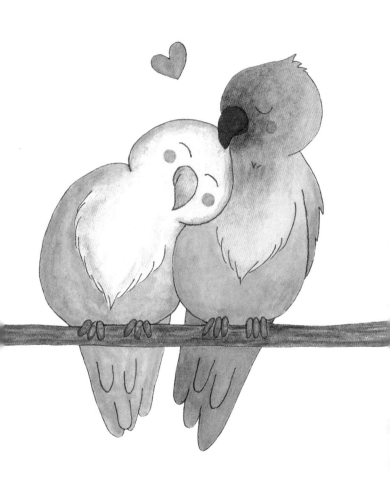

We're tweet-hearts

You're so foxy

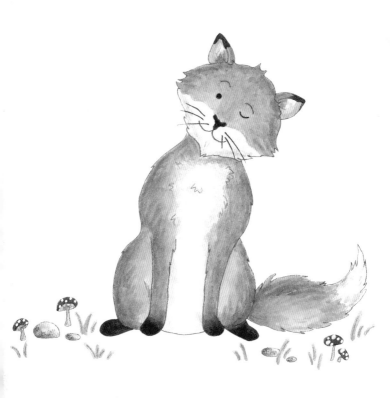

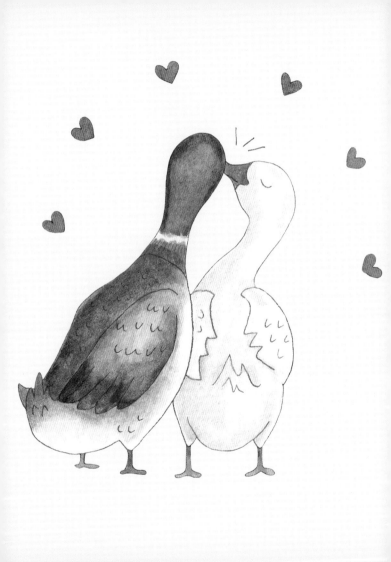

Kiss me quack

I moose you when
we're apart

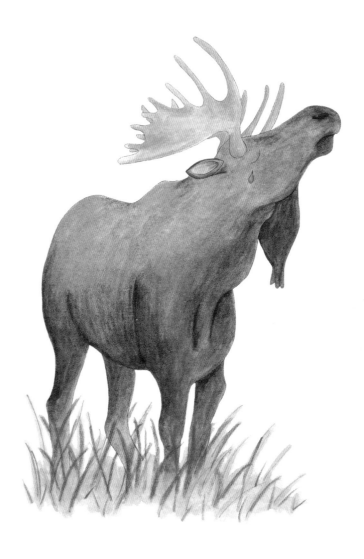

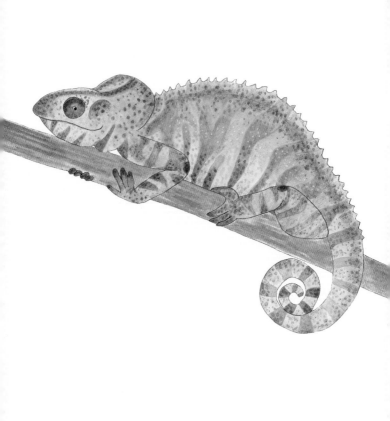

You are one in
a chameleon

Waddle I do without you?

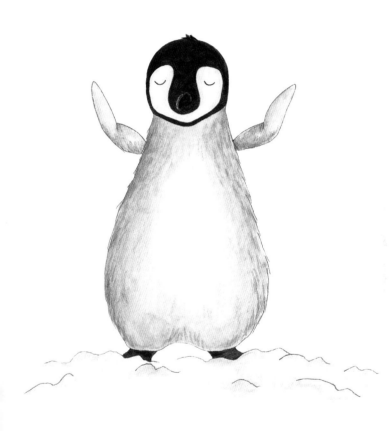

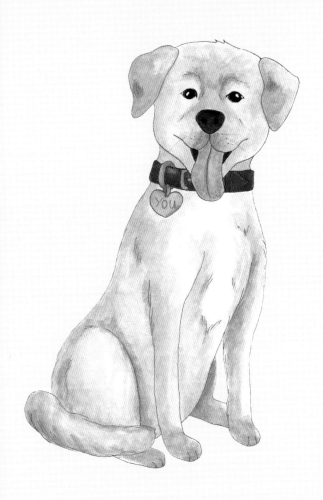

I labr-adore
you

I will always
kanga-root
for you

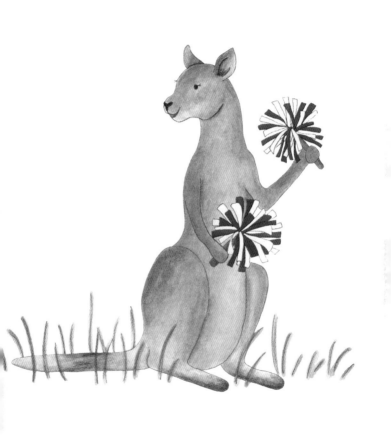

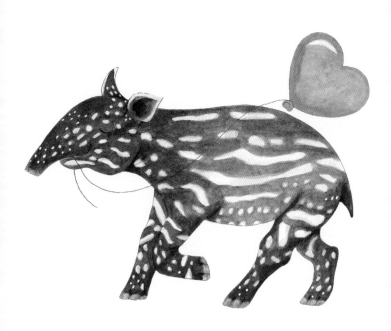

May our love never
tapir off

Llama love you
forever

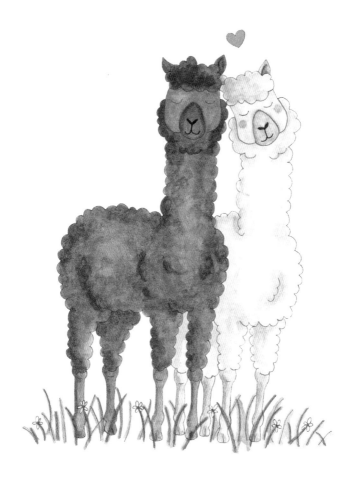

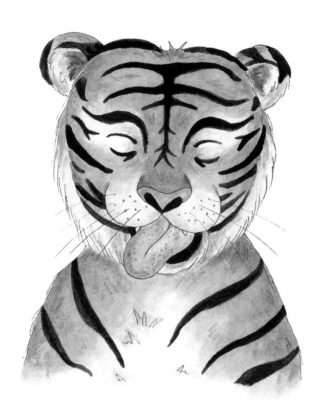

You're
roar-some

You've got my
seal of approval

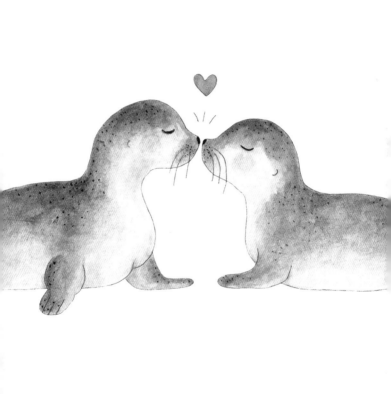

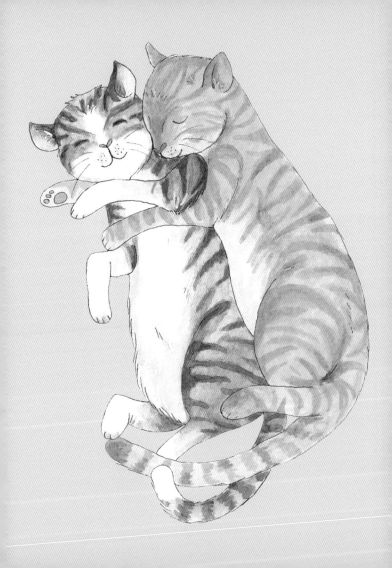

Always yours,
meow and forever

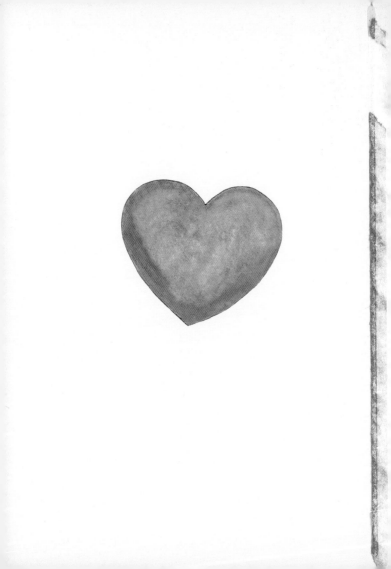